ONCE·UPON·A·TIMES·TABLE

Laurence Shaw

PICTURES BY
FRANCIS MOSLEY

Kingfisher Books

How to read this book

Once Upon A Times Table consists of eleven stories, one for each of the multiplication tables from 2 to 12. "Double or Nothing", for example, is the story of Quentin and the two times table. Like the other stories, it is divided into 12 parts, and you must know the answer to each part of the table and turn to that page in order to follow the story. $2 \times 2 = 4$, go to page 4; $2 \times 3 = 6$, go to page 6, and so on...

To Quentin, who finally learned them, and Leona, who, because she learned them so quickly, never gave me the opportunity to write a book for her.

First published in 1985 by Kingfisher Books Limited
Elsley Court, 20–22 Great Titchfield Street London W1P 7AD
A Grisewood & Dempsey Company

Text Copyright © Laurence Shaw 1985
Illustrations Copyright © Kingfisher Books Limited 1985

BRITISH LIBRARY CATALOGUING IN PUBLICATION DATA
Shaw, Laurence
    Once upon a times table.
    1. Multiplication-Juvenile literature
    I. Title
    513'.2 QA115
    ISBN 0 86272 140 7

Printed in Italy by Vallardi Industrie Grafiche, Milan

ONCE UPON A TIMES TABLE

This book is about a little boy called Quentin. Quentin went to school and had lots of maths lessons. First he learnt how to add, and then he learnt how to subtract. Quentin liked playing with numbers, and he tried very hard to learn his times tables. But multiplication was more difficult than adding up or taking away. Perhaps numbers were not such fun after all . . . Then, one day, something extraordinary happened which made Quentin see numbers quite differently.

Once upon a times table, Quentin went to bed – and thought he fell asleep. But he had no sooner closed his eyes than . . . Turn the page.

2

**Double
or Nothing**

$$1 \times 2 = 2$$

Quentin found himself in a strange land where everything was in pairs. Two cars raced past him on two roads.

Two trees gave twice as much shade from two suns in the sky. Quentin had heard of seeing double but this was ridiculous! Feeling rather dazed, he decided to sit down in one of the two chairs in front of him – and found himself in both.

Suddenly, with two mighty roars, two gigantic monsters came crashing through the trees. Quentin's heart missed a couple of beats and he gave two great gulps as they came towards him. Just then, two little birds flew from a nearby tree and landed on two laser guns which lay on the ground next to him.

"2×2, 2×2, hurry!" they cheeped.

(Now work out what 2×2 is and turn to the page the answer gives you.)

3 The Three Times Bears

$$1 \times 3 = 3$$

Having finished the two times table, Quentin decided he would never have anything to do with twos again. He was just looking round for a place to sit down when there were three taps on his shoulder.

"Excuse me, young man," said a gruff voice, "can you help us?"

"Oh no," thought Quentin, "here we go again. Off to 2×3."

3

4 The Story of the Four-sided Quadrangler

1×4=4

Have you ever heard of the four-sided Quadrangler? It's a strange sea-creature, not a fish, and certainly not a seaweed – in fact it's not really like anything else at all. Nobody has ever seen it except Quentin, but it's there under the water, and will tell you it's sad story if you meet it when you're swimming.

One day in the holidays, Quentin was diving off the coast with his new goggles and a straw he used as a snorkel. He looked down through the clear water and saw a very odd-looking creature. He had no idea what it was, so he went on to 2×4.

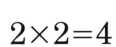

2×2=4

"2×2=4!" shouted Quentin. A red light came on in each of the laser guns. He quickly picked them up and pressed the triggers. With two blinding flashes, the monsters went up in two puffs of smoke.

"Phew, that was close!" he gasped.

"Your troubles aren't over yet, young man," piped the birds. Quentin looked down and groaned. Two snakes were gradually winding their way up his legs.

"Try 3×2, Quentin," the birds called as they flew away.

5 Sir Quentin and the Crazy Confused Dragon

$$1 \times 5 = 5$$

Sir Quentin was having a bad day.

It was extremely hot and he was not enjoying galloping all over the countryside in his steaming armour.

He had not seen any dragons for months. The only good thing was that he was on page 5, which was his favourite page because Quentin comes from the latin word for five. With the name Quentin he just couldn't help being good at the five times table.

"I'm going to gallop through this table and find a dragon if it's the last thing I do," he told himself fiercely. And off he went, with a sharp command to his horse, Leonalli, "2×5 and away!"

6 The Case of the Mad Sexapod

$$1\times6=6$$

There once lived a mad sexapod on the planet Arfadozen. It was quite harmless, but often changed into the strangest shapes and turned the most extraordinary colours. Quentin knew nothing about this as he prepared to land his spaceship on the planet Arfadozen one day.

"Engines one sixth speed, go to 2×6," he ordered.

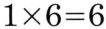

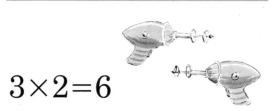

$$3\times2=6$$

Since $3\times2=6$, $2\times3=6$ and $1\times6=6$, Quentin decided that the way to escape the snakes was to hop over into another times table. He chose the three times table, because 3×2 and 2×3 are really the same thing. Hop! And when he hopped back, the snakes had gone.

"On to 4×2," cried the birds.

$$2\times3=6$$

Quentin turned and saw 6 bears.

"Shouldn't you be 3 bears?" he asked. "Like in the story . . ."

"We *were* 3 bears," answered one of the daddy bears, "before you brought us to this page. Anyway, if there are two of you, why shouldn't there be six of us?"

Quentin swung round and found himself face to face with Quentin from the two times table who had just jumped into the three times table to escape the snakes.

"Hello and goodbye," said Quentin to Quentin, and jumped back to 3×2. Quentin turned to the daddy bears.

"You asked for my help. What can I do for you?"

"Go to 3×3 and I'll tell you," answered daddy bear one.

7 Wishing by Numbers

$1 \times 7 = 7$

Quentin liked the number seven. He was 7 years old, and he knew that there were seven days in a week and he was born on the seventh. So he was pleased when he reached seven in his times tables, and very cross when he couldn't remember what to do.

"I wish I knew what 2×7 is," he muttered.

8

The Lazy Octopus

$$1 \times 8 = 8$$

There was turmoil at Octopusal Mansions. Octavia was having one of her tantrums.

"It's about time somebody taught that octopus a lesson," grumbled the neighbours. For Octavia was the laziest octopus in the world. Today's argument had started when her mother told her to tidy her room.

"It won't take long if you use all your legs at once," she said cheerfully.

At the thought of using all her legs at once, Octavia flew into a rage. She shouted and stamped, and flounced off to her room.

"If only I was grown up," she howled, "then nobody could tell me what to do. I wish I was 2×8, not just 8!"

$$4 \times 2 = 8$$

This time Quentin landed in a field in which stood two fearsome great bulls. They blinked wildly at him, snorted, and, with one accord, came charging towards him.

"You'd better scarper!" called the birds, "5×2, and hurry!"

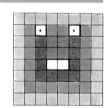

$$2 \times 4 = 8$$

"What can it be?" he pondered, peering at the creature. "I'm not sure I like the look of it much."

"How rude! Things are bad enough without people thinking such nasty thoughts." Quentin twirled round in the water to see who was saying these bubbly words. He saw no one, so he tried 3×4.

9 Qat's Nine Lives

$1 \times 9 = 9$

"It's hard work having nine lives, you know," Qat observed to Quentin as they were having a game of ninepins in the garden one day. With a graceful swing, he threw the ball and knocked down 2×9 ninepins in one go.

$3 \times 3 = 9$

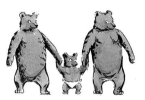

"That's better," said daddy bear one. "More peaceful on this page. Bears like a quiet life, you know."

"I'm sure they do," agreed Quentin. "But what exactly was it you wanted to ask me?"

"We are lost in the forest and can't find our way home," one of the two mummy bears explained.

"I expect I can help," smiled Quentin. "I know this forest backwards because I've been running through it all day escaping from

monsters, snakes, mad bulls and space invaders." At these words, the six bears screamed and tried to jump into each other others' arms.

"It's alright, they've all gone now," Quentin reassured them, although he was still quite afraid himself. "Let's go on to 4×3."

9

10

10 O'clock and Still Not Asleep

$1 \times 10 = 10$

One summer holiday the strangest thing happened to Quentin. It was the summer he went to Portugal and stayed in a little hotel surrounded by orchards of almond trees. All day he played in the garden, and when he was too hot he dived into the pool to cool off.

The nights were hot and very sticky. Quentin was usually tired after playing all day, but one night he just couldn't get to sleep. He tossed and turned, as he lay counting the chirpings of the crickets. He counted 2×10.

$5 \times 2 = 10$

Quentin found himself in another part of the country. There were still two of everything – but no bulls.

"That's better," he sighed, and looked round for a place to rest. But the two little birds called,

"Keep moving, Quentin, 6×2!"

$2 \times 5 = 10$

As Sir Quentin was galloping through the countryside, a crazy dragon in a dark, moist cave deep beneath the black mountain was busy shampooing her hair and drying it with her fiery breath.

"How beautiful I am," she thought, as she looked in her mirror. "I am a most beautiful princess." Meanwhile Sir Quentin was up to 3×5.

11 Quentin's Mysterious Friend

$$1 \times 11 = 11$$

One winter's evening, Quentin was sitting in the sitting room, warm and snug in front of the fire. Sunk in an armchair with one leg hanging over its side, he gazed into the flickering flames, dreaming of warmer places in the sun. How he'd like to be on a beach making sandcastles!

"You enjoy that sort of thing, but it's not much fun for me." Quentin looked around in astonishment. Surely there was no one else in the room?

"I'm here behind you." Quentin swung round but there was no one there.

"I'm sorry, I can't see you," he said.

"Of course you can," he was told. "Just like the number eleven – wherever you go, I go."

"I don't understand."

"Well, what do you notice about 2×11?"

12 They Went in Twelve by Twelve

$1 \times 12 = 12$

It had been one of those days for Noah. You know the sort I mean, when nothing ever goes right. And now the sky was darkening by the minute and it was certain to rain. He called his three sons to tell them it was time to round up all the animals. And before he could forget – because he had a terrible memory – Noah tied a knot in his beard to remind himself to buy buns for the elephants.

"Would 2×12 be enough?" he wondered. How many was that?

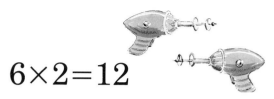

$6 \times 2 = 12$

But when he got there he found himself squashed between two other stories.

"Surely these times tables don't all make 12!" gasped Quentin, gazing out over the crowded page. He decided to hurry on to 7×2, and he didn't even wait for the birds to cheep.

$4 \times 3 = 12$

"This is a crowded place," whimpered baby bear number one. "I don't like it here at all."

"Don't worry, baby bear," said Quentin. "As soon as I've worked out 5×3, we'll be off."

$3 \times 4 = 12$

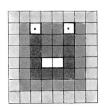

But there was no one or rather nothing there except the creature.

"I'm a four-sided Quadrangler and I can read people's thoughts," the bubbly voice began again. "Go to 4×4 and I'll tell you more."

$2 \times 6 = 12$

The engines slowed and the spaceship went into orbit around Arfadozen.

"Prepare to beam down," Quentin ordered the ship's computers.

"Ready at 3×6," came the automatic reply.

12

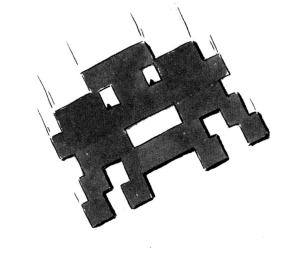

$7 \times 2 = 14$

"More room at last," said Quentin. "And there isn't a 14 times table."

"Who says there isn't?" boomed two very deep voices. Quentin looked up.

"Oh no!" he shrieked. Hurtling down at him were the two biggest, blackest space invaders he'd ever seen.

"Don't argue with them, Quentin. Just hurry to 8×2," called the birds.

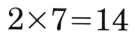

$2 \times 7 = 14$

"$2 \times 7 = 14$!" He knew the answer at once. "That's lucky," thought Quentin, "or could it be magic . . ? Whatever it is, I wish I knew 3×7!"

14

$5 \times 3 = 15$

"Isn't that our house through the trees?" cried mummy bear number one at last. "What a clever young man you are!" Quentin felt very pleased with himself.

"6×3 and we're there," he told the bears proudly.

$3 \times 5 = 15$

Sir Quentin arrived at the foot of a black mountain.

"There must be a dragon here!" he cried. Then he sniffed the air and made a face, "Funny smell, though . . . like burning hair."

"Uhm," agreed Leonalli, who never said very much. Suddenly, they heard a terrible noise.

"Great gorodkins!" shrieked Sir Quentin. "And 4×5."

8×2=16

Faster than a flash, Quentin leapt over page 15 and landed on this page with a shout of "8×2=16!" He was in good company: 2×8 and 4×4 had already arrived.

"It's exciting, but I'm beginning to feel a little tired," puffed Quentin.

"Keep going," the birds chirped. "You're almost there. On to 9×2."

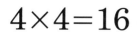

4×4=16

"But how can I hear you?" thought Quentin.

"That's easy. I can send messages through the water like electric waves. You pick them up with your skin, then the electricity travels along the nerves to your brain and it seems as though you actually heard them. I'm sending one now, for instance. 5×4."

$2 \times 8 = 16$

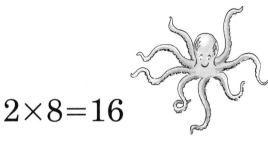

Octavia would have to wait a long time before she was sixteen, and her parents were determined to cure her of her laziness before then. Her father decided that there was only one thing to do: he must consult the Wise Whale. So he made himself a big pile of seaweed sandwiches in case he got hungry on the journey, and he took his old compass from the hall table. He was just setting off when he remembered he had no idea where the Wise Whale lived – and he hadn't seen him for 3×8 years.

$9 \times 2 = 18$

At page 18 the road branched in different directions and Quentin had no idea which way to go. There was no one about except an old man snoozing under a tree. Quentin went over and shook him very gently.

"Can you tell me which way to go for the two times table, please?" The old man woke with a start, then he scratched his head and admitted that he couldn't remember.

"Try that one," he said at last, pointing with his stick. "It's as likely to lead to 10×2 as the other one." There was no arguing with that, so off Quentin went.

$6 \times 3 = 18$

And of course they were.

"Please come in, young man," said mummy bear number two.

"I can't open the door," grumbled daddy bear number one, tugging at the handle. "It must have got stuck."

"Try 7×3," suggested Quentin.

$3 \times 6 = 18$

Quentin landed on Arfadozen. He pressed a button on his wrist to let the spaceship's computer know his position.

"You can find me on 4×6," he told it.

$2 \times 9 = 18$

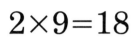

"So many more things happen in nine lives than in one. In my last life I was a cat burglar with a terrible fear of heights. Cat-astrophe! One night I found myself clinging for my dear eighth life to a window ledge on the 27th floor. 'Help!' I shouted. 'Dial 999!'"

"You mean 3×9," said Quentin, "which is . . ."

18

$10 \times 2 = 20$

The old man had guessed right: Quentin found himself on page 20.

"Only two more twos to go!" he called brightly to the two birds. "See you at 11×2."

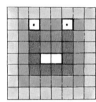

$5 \times 4 = 20$

"At first I used to be round not square," the Quadrangler went on. "I wasn't called Quadrangler then and I couldn't read minds or send messages through water onto people's skins. Then something awful happened. Go to 6×4 and I'll tell you about it."

$4 \times 5 = 20$

The horrible noise Sir Quentin heard was the crazy dragon singing as she singed her hair. She thought she had an exquisite voice – but then she had never heard herself sing (or anyone else for that matter).

"Strange noise for a dragon," observed Quentin.

"Uhm," replied Leonalli.

"Still, I don't see what else it can be," said Sir Quentin. He saw the dark mouth of a cave ahead. The noise seemed to be coming from inside. Sir Quentin raised his lance and urged Leonalli towards the entrance.

"Forever onwards!" he cried. "5×5!"

$2 \times 10 = 20$

Twenty chirpings . . . or is it chirps? Anyway, Quentin had counted up to 20 of them, when suddenly he heard another noise. It was a sort of whirring noise, and it seemed to be coming from inside his room, which was very strange because Quentin was quite alone.

He turned over in bed and looked around. To his amazement, in the moonlight he could see a little pile of sawdust forming in the middle of the floor. It looked like a picture of a pyramid in Egypt that Quentin had seen. The whirring sound came from the pile of sawdust. Suddenly out of it popped something black, round and shiny.

"Well, I'll be 3×10!" exclaimed Quentin.

20

$7 \times 3 = 21$

The handle turned and they all went into the house. Daddy bear number one was just about to sit down when he stopped and gave a great growl.

"Who's been sitting in my chair?"

"You mean *my* chair," scowled daddy bear number two.

"I think I know," said Quentin brightly. "What are 8×3?"

$3 \times 7 = 21$

"$3 \times 7 = 21 \ldots$ it must be magic! That means I can make a wish every time I say the seven times table!" With great excitement, Quentin closed his eyes, crossed his fingers, rubbed his nose and thought hard. "4×7, 4×7, I wish I was on the moon!"

21

$11 \times 2 = 22$

"Nothing can stop me now!" cried Quentin, barely pausing before he shot on to 12×2.

$2 \times 11 = 22$

"2×11," said Quentin, "Why that's 22!"

"Exactly," answered the voice. "And what's special about 22?" Quentin thought very hard.

"Nothing, as far as I can see," he said at last, "and talking of seeing, where are you?"

"Right behind you," said the voice wearily. "There's obviously something special about 22, and I can't believe you don't see it. Try again." Quentin racked his brain. $11 \times 2 = 22$ and $2 \times 11 = 22$ but no other times table would divide into it. If there was a 22 times table, then $1 \times 22 = 22$, and if the times tables went on further than 12, then $22 \times 1 = 22$ in the one times table might be interesting . . . But none of this gave him a clue to the identity of the mysterious voice.

"I really don't know," sighed Quentin after another long pause, in which there was no sound but the crackling of the fire.

"Well, try 3×11 then," the voice said impatiently.

22

$12 \times 2 = 24$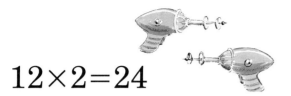

"Wow! What a very crowded page!" exclaimed Quentin.

"So why are you taking up so much room?" chirped the birds.

"I won't for much longer," answered Quentin. "I've finished the two times table and I'm going to stop, so I won't take up any room at all."

"Oh, but you haven't finished," chorused the birds. "You've only just started. Go to page 3."

$6 \times 4 = 24$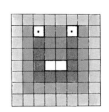

"I was rolling along the bottom of the sea one day, minding my own business, when a strong current suddenly caught me up and swept me along. It happened so quickly that I crashed into a huge rock almost before I knew it. I flopped down on the sand unable to move, and then I saw it coming towards me . . . 7×4."

$8 \times 3 = 24$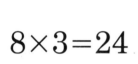

"It must have been the wolf," Quentin announced.

"The wolf? There's no wolf in this story!" objected daddy bear number one. But he was wrong!

"I think I'm getting muddled," said Quentin. "Let's try 9×3."

$4\times6=24$

It was difficult to move in his spacesuit, but as he turned, he found a horrible-looking creature staring up at him.

"Ugh!" Quentin exclaimed.

"5×6," said the creature brightly.

$3\times8=24$

24 years is a very long time. The Wise Whale would be very old by now, if he was still alive. For what seemed like ages, Octavia's father travelled here and there across the sea floor, but he found no trace of the Wise Whale. At last, tired and hungry, he sat down on a rock and opened his sandwiches. As he did so, he noticed a great crack in the rock and, when he looked more closely, he discovered it was the entrance to a tunnel. An arrow carved on the wall read, '4×8 is . . .'

$2\times12=24$

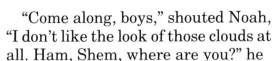

"Come along, boys," shouted Noah, "I don't like the look of those clouds at all. Ham, Shem, where are you?" he called, stamping his foot. But his sons took their time because Noah was always calling for them and then forgetting what he wanted them for. Eventually they strolled out of the house. Japhet was singing,

"3×12 is, 3×12 is . . ." But he didn't know the answer. Do you?

the fairy princess?" You see, not only did this crazy dragon think she was a princess – she thought she was a fairy princess as well.

The dreadful noise she made frightened Leonalli, who neighed and reared up on his hind legs. Any other knight would have told his horse to calm down and given it a sweet. Sir Quentin fell off instead. He had never been a very good rider, and he was even worse at getting on a horse, particularly when wearing all his armour. He tried getting on sideways, but he slipped over to the other side; then from behind, but he missed.

"Oh, blast and 6×5!" he said in a very hot and bothered voice.

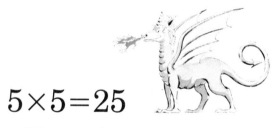

$5 \times 5 = 25$

"I have a whole page for the battle, so come out and fight, you cowardly dragon," Sir Quentin shouted at the hole in the mountain. The noise stopped. "I'm glad you've stopped making that revolting noise," he added. From deep inside the mountain came an almighty roar.

"Revolting noise! Revolting noise!" howled the dragon. "Who dares insult

$9 \times 3 = 27$

"If it wasn't the wolf, I wonder who did sit in your chair," mused Quentin.

"I've no idea, but they've eaten all my porridge as well!" cried daddy bear number one furiously.

"And mine," said daddy bear number two.

"And mine," chorused mummy bear numbers one and two.

"And mine," cried baby bear number one. But baby bear number two said nothing at all.

"Why is he so quiet?" Quentin wondered. "Could it be . . ?"

Go to 10×3 to see what Quentin was thinking.

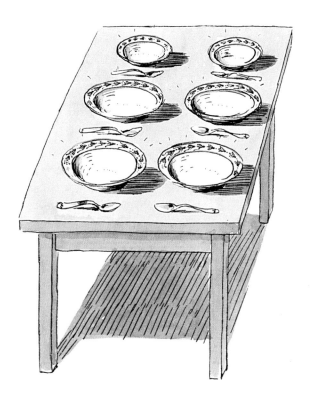

$3 \times 9 = 27$

"Nobody came. I lost my grip and plunged to my next life – which is why I'm here. In the life before that I went to London to visit the Queen."

"And what did you do there?" Quentin asked.

"I stupidly and most unwisely frightened her favourite pet mouse from under her chair. 'Arrest that murderous mog!' she commanded. 'Chop off his head before I can say 4×9 is dirty tricks.' "

27

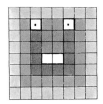

$7 \times 4 = 28$

"What?" said (or rather thought) Quentin.

"A shark," answered the Quadrangler, and it bubbled terribly. "The thought of it still makes me quake with fear."

"What did you do?"

"What would you have done in my place?"

"I'd have tried 8×4."

"That," said the Quadrangler, "is exactly what I did."

$4 \times 7 = 28$

And there he was, standing on the moon in his spacesuit! He was surrounded by craters of all shapes and sizes, but every time he tried to explore, he floated off the ground.

"Of course, there's less gravity here," Quentin realized. "Only a sixth as much as there is on Earth." He noticed a dial that looked like a watch on his wrist and peered at it. 'Oxygen level 2: DANGER!' it flashed. "Oh no, I'm running out of oxygen!" he cried. "5×7, I wish I was back home!"

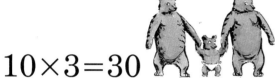

$10 \times 3 = 30$

"It must be baby bear number two!" he cried. The other bears looked round at baby bear number two, but baby bear number two had vanished. Quentin and the other bears rushed upstairs. They looked in all the rooms

and searched under the beds and in the cupboards. Where was baby bear number two?

"11×3 will give me the answer," Quentin decided.

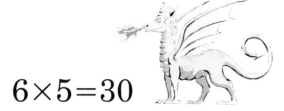

$6 \times 5 = 30$

At last Sir Quentin managed to scramble onto Leonalli's back. The dragon had come out of her cave and was watching his struggles, shaking and snorting with laughter.

"What's so funny?" he snapped.

"Ho, ho, ho!" laughed the dragon.

"7×5," snarled Sir Quentin.

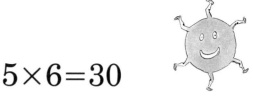

$5 \times 6 = 30$

"What was that?" asked Quentin.

"I said $5 \times 6 = 30$. It's the same as $6 \times 5 = 30$ or $10 \times 3 = 30$ or $3 \times 10 = 30$," the creature chanted smugly.

"Can't you say anything else?" frowned Quentin.

"I can say 6×6," said the creature, "but you'll have to find me there."

$3 \times 10 = 30$

Attached to the round, black, shiny thing was a long spiral which was whirling like a drill. It was the head of a small, brown, furry creature with two rather sad-looking black eyes.

"Good evening," it said pleasantly to Quentin. "What is 4×10?"

30

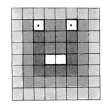

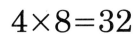

8×4=32

"I thought 8×4=32, and I thought that if I said it often enough I'd turn into an octopus with eight legs to swim away with," said the Quadrangler.

"And did you?"

"No," it sighed.

"Oh dear . . . and what happened then?" asked Quentin.

"There was only one thing I could do. I said 9×4."

4×8=32

'. . . 32 paces to the Wise Whale.' Father Octopus was so excited that he didn't even bother to finish his sandwiches. He set off down the tunnel, counting his paces. When he reached 32, he found himself in a vast underwater cave.

"This must be where the Wise Whale lives," he thought, so he called out, "Is anybody there?" in a loud voice. The sound echoed round the cave but there was no answer. "I think I'll just have 5×8 winks while I wait," he said to himself.

11×3=33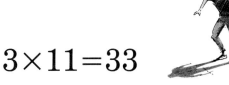

Quentin rushed to baby bear number two's bed, pulled back the covers and there he was! Quentin stared down at his long silvery tail. But bears don't have tails . . !

Baby bear number two squealed and jumped out of bed. He peeled off a furry mask to reveal a rather hot, sweating, uncomfortable little wolf.

"Phew, I'm glad to be out of that! But it was lovely porridge . . ." he called as he disappeared to 12×3.

3×11=33

"So far, the 11 times table all ends in two of the same number, doesn't it?" asked Quentin thoughtfully. "33, 22, 11 . . ."

"Precisely." The voice sounded relieved that he had worked this out. "Now do you know who I am?"

"I've got it!" cried Quentin, "You must be me! You're behind me. You're my shadow."

"At last! I was beginning to think you'd never get there. And it's no fun being a shadow, let me tell you."

"Why ever not?" asked Quentin.

"Try 4×11 and I'll tell you."

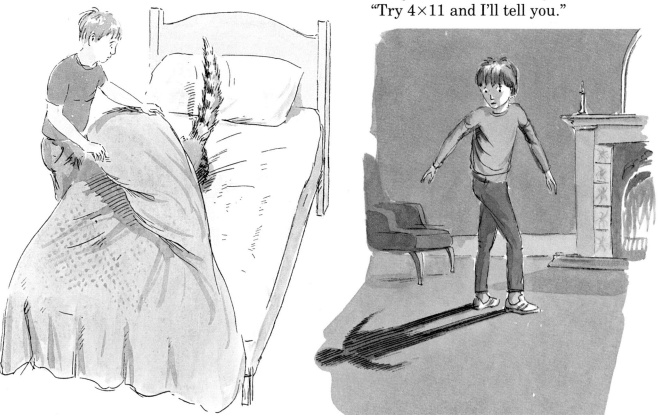

$7\times5=35$

"You look so funny!" shrieked the dragon.

"Well what about you?" Sir Quentin retorted crossly. The dragon stopped laughing and stared at him.

"Me? What about me?" she asked.

"What do you call that?" sneered Sir Quentin, pointing to the dragon's latest hair-do – a heap of messy, rather burnt-looking curls.

"A princess should always look nice," said the dragon primly.

"Princess!" Quentin burst out laughing. Angrily, the dragon roared out a challenge,

"8×5!"

$5\times7=35$

He found himself back in his room at home. On the wall opposite his bed hung a poster showing the solar system with all the planets in orbit around the Sun. It even showed Halley's comet zooming from outer space on its long, slanting orbit. Quentin was particularly fascinated by the red spot of Jupiter. Can you guess what he wished next? Go to 6×7 and find out.

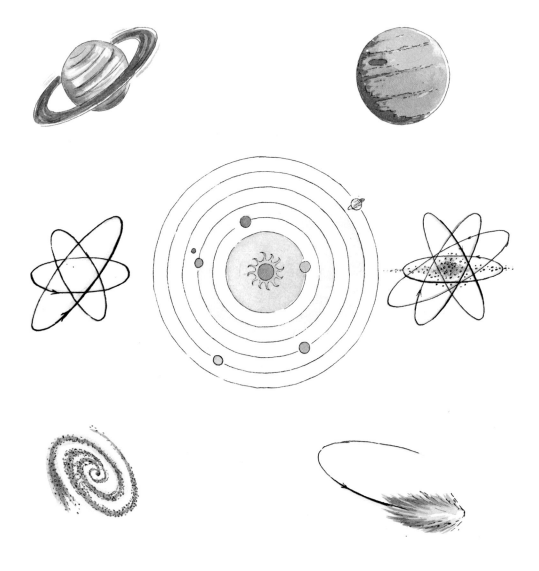

12×3=36

Quentin dashed after the wolf, but he had disappeared into the forest. When he went back to the house, the five bears welcomed him like an old friend.

"We've got a spare bed now," smiled daddy bear number one, "so please come and stay with us any time. But first you must go to page 4 for your next adventure."

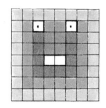

9×4=36

"And then I blew out as hard as I could."

"What did that do?" asked Quentin.

"I got smaller and flatter and managed to slip into a crack at the bottom of the rock."

"Just in time," Quentin observed.

"Yes," sighed the Quadrangler. "And then I said 10×4."

6×6=36

And Quentin did. The creature was already chanting again,

"6×6=36, 12×3=36, 9×4=36, 4×9=36." Suddenly it floated away, went purple and turned inside out. "I can even say 7×6, which is not an easy one to remember," it shouted down. Quentin thought very hard.

"Got it," he called, "7×6 is . . ."

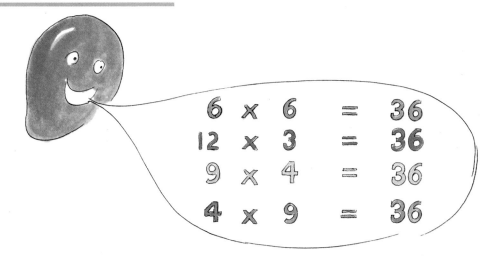

6	x	6	=	36
12	x	3	=	36
9	x	4	=	36
4	x	9	=	36

36

$$4 \times 9 = 36$$

"Dirty tricks . . . thirty six!" Quentin guessed.

"Of course," purred Qat and he went on with the story of his lives.

"Before that I was a musician, travelling all over the world and playing my violin. I was so famous that someone wrote a poem about me which begins 'Hey diddle diddle, the cat and the fiddle' . . . That life came to an end one day when a lady who didn't like my music poured a bucket of water over me and I caught a very bad cold. I must have sneezed at least 5×9 times before I died."

$$3 \times 12 = 36$$

"Ah, there you are," said Noah. "Now, what was I going to say? All of a sudden it's gone right out of my head." The three sons groaned simultaneously. They were just about to go away again when Noah remembered what he wanted to say.

"Ah, yes. It's time to fetch the animals before those clouds break and we all get soaked. Ham, you go and find all the mammals; Shem, you find the birds and Japhet can fetch the reptiles and the slithery things like that. And please be back in time for supper."

"OK, Dad," said Ham, pleased to be able to go out for a change instead of knocking nails into the Ark. "By the way," he added, "why is there a knot in your beard?"

"A knot in my beard," repeated Noah wonderingly. "Why I've no idea, but I must remember to buy some buns for the elephants. 4×12 will do," he thought, stroking his beard. How many buns now?

36

$10 \times 4 = 40$

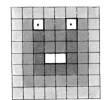

"And the shark swished by and snapped its jaws shut. But I was stuck in the crack in the rock, and all I could do was say 11×4."

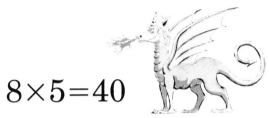

$8 \times 5 = 40$

Sir Quentin lowered his lance.

"8×5 is 40 and so is 5×8!" he cried, digging his heels into Leonalli's sides to start his charge. Leonalli reared up in surprise and threw him on the ground again.

"Ouch and 9×5!" Quentin groaned.

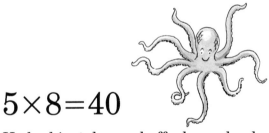

$5 \times 8 = 40$

He had just dropped off when a loud voice rumbled in his ear,

"What can I do for you, young man?" Father Octopus woke up with a start and found himself face to face with a large and venerable whale.

"Oh please, Wise Whale," he cried, "help me to cure my daughter Octavia of her terrible laziness!" The whale looked thoughtful and sighed deeply.

"Give me two days," he said. "That's 6×8 hours."

$4 \times 10 = 40$

"Forty," answered the astonished Quentin. "Who are you, where did you come from, and what are you doing in my room?" he gabbled. The little creature held up its hands to stop the questions.

"I'm a Poggle," it said solemnly, "a Poggle from Poggleland. In answer to your last question, I often come here because, quite simply, I like it here. But I can't stay long tonight, so if you have any other questions, you'd better come with me." Before Quentin could say a word, the Poggle disappeared down the hole, which Quentin now saw was considerably larger than he had at first thought. Without a moment's hesitation, he tumbled forward and found himself falling, falling, falling down the hole. For some strange reason he was saying,

"5×10 is . . ."

$7 \times 6 = 42$

"Is that all you do?" asked Quentin. "Repeat the times tables all the time? I suppose you think it's clever."

"Frankly, I do," replied the creature. "Yes, I must admit, I think I'm very clever."

"And ugly," said Quentin.

"What!" spluttered the creature, dropping quickly to the ground. "Purple is my favourite colour and EVERYONE says how nice I look inside out."

"You look pretty ugly to me." Quentin was not in his politest mood. The creature was very upset and stammered,

"All I can say t-t-t-to you, young man, is . . . is . . . 8×6."

$6 \times 7 = 42$

The next minute Quentin was on the planet Jupiter. There were so many moons in the sky that it was like daylight. Quentin's gaze moved over piles of glowing rocks and he decided to explore. But when he tried to take a step forward, he found he couldn't move. It was gravity, he realized, so much gravity that he couldn't move a muscle. The Moon had had much less gravity than the Earth, which was why he had nearly floated away, but here there was so much more that he couldn't even open his mouth. Quentin thought carefully and then he wished a silent wish.

"7×7, I wish I was a deep-sea diver at the bottom of the sea."

42

$11 \times 4 = 44$

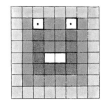

"How did that help?" asked Quentin.

"I knew that going through the 4s had made me flatter already," the Quadrangler explained, "so I kept on saying $11 \times 4 = 44$ until I had said so many 4s that I was as flat as a card and could slip out again."

"Very clever," said Quentin, full of admiration for the little creature.

"Well yes," answered the Quadrangler, "but I forgot something."

"What?"

"Go to 12×4 and I'll tell you."

$4 \times 11 = 44$

"You were remembering that awful holiday by the sea last summer, weren't you?" the shadow began.

"It wasn't awful," said Quentin, "In fact it was the best holiday ever."

"I know," groaned the shadow. "You really enjoyed playing on the beach, jumping into the sea, throwing buckets of water over your sister and that sort of thing. I had to stay on that boiling hot sand all day. It was no fun for me, I can tell you."

"Oh dear," said Quentin, "I never thought of that."

"It's a bit late to feel sorry," retorted

the shadow. "But that wasn't the worst of it."

"Why? What happened?" asked Quentin.

"Well, one day when you had gone swimming I was so uncomfortable that I decided to find somewhere in the shade to escape from the hot sand and sun. Nearby on the beach was a little boy about your size. Just as you went into the sea, he got up from his deckchair and started to walk away."

"What did you do?"

"I performed a special trick using the times table you like best. I whispered '5×11 is the same as 11×5, which is . . .'"

$9 \times 5 = 45$

Sir Quentin lay on the ground for a moment, too stunned to move. Then he tried to pull out his sword, but it was stuck in its scabbard. He tugged and tugged, but it refused to budge. The dragon, who was very cross by this time, came closer and glared down at him.

"Oh no," he moaned, pulling at the sword. "Oh no and 10×5!"

$5 \times 9 = 45$

"The life before that," Qat went on, "I was the proud mascot of a regiment of fine soldiers. I used to sit on the back of the captain's saddle as he rode into battle, and sometimes I would spring up and shock the advancing enemy. Like so many soldiers, I died fighting – in the prime of my cathood, aged 6×9."

12×4=48

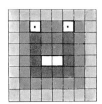

"I forgot that I was now completely flat. I had used the number 4 so many times that I was now a very strange 4-sided Quadrangler."

"Oh dear, I am sorry," said Quentin.

"Thank you for your sympathy," replied the Quadrangler. "And do let me warn you never to change shape if you can help it – even in the next times table which I know is your favourite. Goodbye and good luck!"

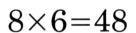

8×6=48

The creature was now green and very flat indeed.

"At least there are plenty of times tables on this page," it muttered. "4×12=48, 12×4=48, 8×6=48, 6×8=48." Quentin didn't know what to do with this times table crazy creature. He just could not have a sensible discussion with it.

"Get it on a page with hardly any times tables," he decided. "9×6."

$6 \times 8 = 48$

Octavia's father went back home and waited patiently until the two days were up. He told nobody where he had been. When he returned to the hidden cave, the Wise Whale was nowhere to be seen. In the middle of the cave was a large octagonal box. Attached to the box was an envelope on which was written "To Mr Octopus". Octavia's father eagerly opened his letter. It didn't take him long to read it, 7×8 seconds to be precise.

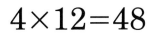

$4 \times 12 = 48$

Noah sat on a rock wondering which shops would be open at this time of day to buy buns. He was soon lost in a daydream and, of course, completely forgot what it was he was thinking about in the first place.

It was not until some time later that a loud rumble disturbed his thoughts. Noah looked up and, to his amazement, he saw $5 \times 12 \ldots$

$7 \times 7 = 49$

No sooner had Quentin wished his silent wish than he found himself at the bottom of the sea in a diving suit and helmet, blowing bubbles all around him. He moved a foot but it plonked back onto the sand in a heavy lead shoe.

Around him swirled sea anemones, a beautiful clown fish, octopusses . . . and a giant squid. A GIANT SQUID! The menacing tentacles slid silently towards him – and suddenly everything went black.

"I'm covered in ink," Quentin realized in a flash. "That must mean those tentacles are very, very near." He closed his eyes and said as quickly and calmly as he could,

"I wish I was a marine biologist, floating safely in a glass bubble. 8×7."

$10 \times 5 = 50$

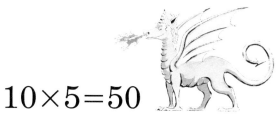

Just then Sir Quentin managed to pull out his sword and scramble to his feet.

"Now we'll see who's a princess!" he shouted defiantly.

"I didn't know *you* were a princess," exclaimed the dragon.

"I'm not, you're the princess, I'm the dragon. No . . . that's not right." Thoroughly confused, he sat down and scratched his helmet. He wanted to scratch his head, but he couldn't with all that armour on.

"You don't know what you're talking about," said the dragon scornfully. "I've always been a fairy princess. I'm not sure what you are, but you don't look like anything much at all. I can't believe you're a princess too. Come on, tell me the truth or I'll . . . I'll . . . 11×5!"

$5 \times 10 = 50$

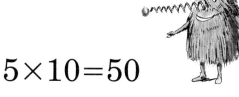

Quentin came to a stop with a gentle thud. He had landed on a very soft cushion in what seemed to be a glass dome. If it hadn't been so dark outside, he would have been able to see out in every direction. There was a complicated control panel on which the Poggle was already busy pressing buttons and turning small wheels. Red, green and blue lights flashed and a low buzzing noise seemed to come from below him. Suddenly the dome turned green.

"Hang on tight!" shouted the Poggle and before Quentin had time to answer, the Poggle train – for that is what it was – shot forward at fantastic speed. It seemed to be travelling in a tunnel. 6×10! Woosh!

50

9×6=54

The creature scowled at Quentin.

"Clever, aren't you?" it said. "But just because you've got me on this page doesn't mean this is the end, you know." Quentin looked the creature up and down. It was no longer flat; in fact, it was almost circular.

"What are you?" he asked.

"I'm a sexapod," said the creature, "which means that I love the six times table. There are only a few of us left in the entire Universe and we all live here on Arfadozen. And even here there are only 10×6 of us."

6×9=54

"Long, long ago – it must have been in my fourth life – I earned my living as a ratcatcher, going from town to town. One place I remember particularly well was the city of Hamelin in Germany, where there was a terrible plague of the little creatures," Qat wrinkled his nose at the memory. "Rats! They fought the dogs and killed the cats, bit the babies in their cradles and ate the cheese out of the vats.

"I marched into the city dressed up to the nines in a brightly coloured hat and cloak, and carrying a little reed pipe in my paw. I began to play a tune and, as if by magic, the rats followed me, fat ones and thin ones, brown ones and grey ones. They came from every house in every street in the city, till there was not a single rat left in Hamelin. I led them down to the river and watched as they plunged into the water in their thousands. The people were very grateful and begged me to stay, but I shook the dust from my paws and disappeared to another life."

"7×9?" asked Quentin.

"That's right."

$11\times5=55$

Quentin's head was hurting.

"I'm not a fairy princess," he began wearily, "and neither are you. And I don't understand why you don't want to be a dragon." The dragon looked puzzled. "I mean, why can't you be a dragon princess?"

"A dragon princess and not a fairy princess?" said the crazy dragon thoughtfully.

"That's right."

"Great gorodkins and 12×5!" laughed the dragon. "I never thought of that."

$5\times11=55$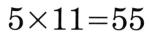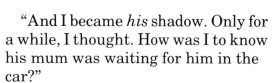

"And I became *his* shadow. Only for a while, I thought. How was I to know his mum was waiting for him in the car?"

"And where was she going?" gasped Quentin.

"A long way away, and she was in a hurry. The boy jumped into the car and she drove off."

"Oh dear!" cried Quentin.

"Oh dear indeed," responded the shadow. "But I had a brilliant idea. On the dashboard is a dial called a rev counter which tells the driver how hard the engine is working. Anything above 50 on the dial is dangerous. So just as we went under a bridge, I jumped onto the dial. The driver looked down and, instead of 6, saw..."

"I know," cried Quentin, "6×11!"

$8 \times 7 = 56$

And there he was, Dr Quentinius Quentin, floating in his glass bubble, which turned out to be a fully equipped underwater laboratory. Safe from the squid, he examined specimens of plankton, seaweeds, snails and unusual fish. He collected samples of sea water in test tubes and added acids to see what would happen. But suddenly there was a violent jolt. The bubble span through the water like a football. When it stopped, it was upside down. Chemicals had spilled everywhere and Quentin's head was hurting.

"Oh dear," he groaned, "I wish I was the right way up. 9×7."

$7 \times 8 = 56$

When Father Octopus had read his letter he laughed and laughed.

"This will cure Octavia of her laziness if anything will," he chuckled. He stepped into the box. Once inside, he could see himself reflected on all eight sides. He saw 8×8 legs.

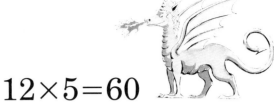

$12 \times 5 = 60$

After that, Quentin and the dragon princess became the best of friends. When he set off on his next adventure, she went with him to the bend in the road, and roared goodbye as he turned the corner to page 6.

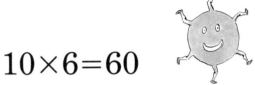

$10 \times 6 = 60$

The sexapod loved this page, surrounded as it was by so many sixes: $5 \times 12 = 60$, $12 \times 5 = 60$, $10 \times 6 = 60$ and $6 \times 10 = 60$. It became quite large and pink with pleasure.

"There's only one page better," it chortled. "11×6 is . . ."

60

$6 \times 10 = 60$

"Where are we going?" yelled Quentin. But the Poggle was far too busy pulling levers and pressing buttons on the control panel to answer. Quentin found his way to a seat and quickly put on a seat belt. It was the most extraordinary train ride he had ever been on. Above, he could see moonlight filtering through water.

"It must be a sea-train!" he exclaimed in wonder. Gradually it got darker, and the Poggle flicked a switch. Large powerful headlights came on, and a voice from the control panel said, "7×10 is . . ."

$5 \times 12 = 60$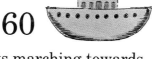

Sixty elephants marching towards him! Sitting on the neck of the first elephant was his son Ham.

"Where shall I take them, Dad?" he shouted down to his father. Before Noah could answer, his son slid off the first elephant's neck and the great herd lumbered on towards the Ark.

"What . . . what . . . what do you call those?"

"Elephants, of course," replied Ham. The elephants climbed into the Ark and stuck their trunks out of the windows.

"No, not them, *them*!" shrieked Noah, pointing into the distance. Ham looked up and saw 6×12 . . .

60

$9 \times 7 = 63$

The glass bubble righted itself. Dr Quentin picked himself up and inspected the damage. The floor was covered in broken test tubes, spilt water and bits of seaweed and rock. Worst of all, a huge sea monster loomed outside the bubble! Dr Quentin turned to the control panel and pressed a red button marked 'Push Me'. At once a laser beam shot through the water and hit the monster. The monster let out a bubbly roar and loomed closer.

"I wish I had a Zagblatter!" cried Quentin. "10×7."

$7 \times 9 = 63$

"To a wild hillside in the middle of nowhere where my mistress Meg, an ugly old witch, was stirring a huge cauldron.

'Niney niney niney nine,
Niney niney niney nine,'
she chanted. Up popped a quivering, jangling skeleton. My fur stood on end and my claws stuck out. The skeleton pointed a long bony finger at me and shrieked, 'Shoo, cat!' 'On to the broomstick,' ordered my mistress, 'and we'll fly to the devil.' Well, I told you I have no head for heights, and that was another life gone. As I fell, I could hear Meg spurring her broomstick, '8×9, 8×9. Hurry!' "

$8 \times 8 = 64$

Father Octopus gazed at his reflections in the eight walls of the glass box, and he smiled to himself.

He dragged the box from the cave and found a friendly clown fish who agreed to deliver it to Octavia the next day.

When the clown fish rang the bell at Octopusal Mansions the next morning, it was Octavia who answered the door.

"Are you an octopus?" asked the fish.

"Don't be a clown," snapped Octavia. "What do I look like? A lobster?"

"I'm sorry," said the fish, "but that's exactly what I am – a clown. Anyway I have a delivery for you." Octavia's eyes nearly popped out of her head when she saw the box.

"How do you open it?" she asked.

"With one more turn of the key than there are sides," replied the fish. How many was that? Turn to 9×8 for the answer.

$11 \times 6 = 66$

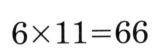

"Oh, it's lovely here," cried the sexapod, and turned a magnificent cartwheel using six little legs with bright purple shoes on that Quentin had not noticed before.

"Why, oh why, do you like the times tables so much?" pleaded Quentin.

"Because . . . well . . . don't you know . . . heehee . . . ho . . . ho . . . ho!" and it lay on the ground howling with laughter. From time to time it spluttered, "12×6, 12×6!"

"I must know the answer," thought Quentin and off he went to 12×6.

$6 \times 11 = 66$

"You *are* a clever boy," said the shadow looking rather surprised.

"It's nothing," Quentin answered modestly.

"The driver quickly put on the brakes and stopped the car. At that moment, a lorry came trundling past in the opposite direction and I shouted to its shadow for help. We shadows always stick together, you know.

"And did the lorry carry you back the beach?"

"Oh yes, and more," laughed the shadow. "The lorry shadow and I had such a good time that we shot past the beach . . . I thought we'd only gone 7 kilometres, but I forgot that road signs aren't shadows and that it wasn't 7 but 7×11 kilometres."

$10 \times 7 = 70$

Looking down, Quentin saw a green button marked 'Zagblatter'. Quickly he pressed it, and a sticky green fluid seeped from the sides of the bubble, covering the monster just as it reached out its seven deadly tentacles.

"Ugh! It tastes like spinach and mouldy cheese – and it's the worst smell in the world," spluttered the monster drawing back in disgust. Whereupon it shook its tentacles so violently that the bubble was sent spinning through the water again. This time it was heading straight for a wall of solid rock.

"I wish it would stop. 11×7!" screamed Quentin.

ZAGBLATTER

$7 \times 10 = 70$

The Poggle train moved at incredible speed through the water. It zoomed between a shark and the small fish it was about to gobble up, almost chopping off the shark's snout. The shark quickly swam off in the opposite direction, leaving the little fish alone.

After a while, the Poggle started to pull levers and press buttons again. The Poggle train slowed down and, looking ahead, Quentin saw a huge rock in the centre of which a concrete door was sliding open. The control panel went red and the whirring noise stopped. They slid silently through the door and everything went black.

"Don't worry," the Poggle reassured Quentin, "they have to let the water out of this chamber before we can go inside."

"Who has to?" asked Quentin.

"The other Poggles, of course," answered the Poggle. In front of them, a shaft of light gradually increased in size as another door opened.

"8×10 . . . continue," said the voice from the control panel.

$12 \times 6 = 72$

"Guess!" cried the sexapod. Quentin thought it over.

"I'm not sure," he said at last, "but it may be because you're good at times tables that you like them so much."

"Yes, that's it!" the sexapod jumped up and down on all six legs at once. Then it stopped suddenly. "But that's all I'm good at," it whispered with tears in its eyes.

Quentin put his arm round it, "Better to be good at something than nothing at all. And you are very good indeed." The sexapod was comforted and smiled a watery smile. He waved as Quentin climbed into his spaceship and took off for page 7.

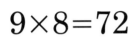

$9 \times 8 = 72$

Turning the key nine times in the lock, Octavia opened the door. It slid silently to one side and she floated into the big box. Suddenly there was a soft hiss and a clunk and the door closed behind her.

"Oh fiddlesticks, now I'm locked in! I shouldn't have gone to all that trouble to open the door in the first place," she muttered peevishly. But then she noticed a parcel on the floor. Perhaps it would help her to find a way out. Octavia settled down to open it, crossing her eight legs ten times each as she tugged at the string. Can you work out how many crosses that is all together? 10×8 is . . .

$8 \times 9 = 72$

"I think the best life I ever had," mused Qat, "was in ancient Egypt long, long ago. People knew how to treat a cat in those days. When I died, everyone in the house cried for weeks on end and the corpse was put in a gold coffin and buried in a special place called a catacomb. Yes, if I had 9×9 lives, I'd choose to spend them all in ancient Egypt." How many lives is that?

$6 \times 12 = 72$

72 zebras!

"Zebras, Dad," Ham told him. "They look rather fine, don't you think?" He was proud to have found so many.

"Like a great pedestrian crossing!" shouted Noah furiously. No sooner were the words out of his mouth than 72 lions and 72 tigers appeared.

"You ham-fisted fool, Ham," he raged, turning redder by the minute. The sky suddenly went very dark. Noah looked up and saw, not only rain clouds, but $7 \times 12 \ldots$

$11 \times 7 = 77$

The bubble stopped slap bang in the middle of the sea, flinging Quentin hard against the glass. He had no time to wish it not to happen. Smash, 12×7!

$7 \times 11 = 77$

"You mean you went 77 kilometres!" gasped Quentin.

"Please don't do that," said the shadow sternly.

"Do what?" asked Quentin.

"Move. If you do, I have to too, and I was just getting comfortable."

"I'm sorry," said Quentin, sitting down again quickly.

"I should think so too," grunted the shadow. "Well, now I was in real trouble because I knew you'd want to come out of the sea soon and that you couldn't without a shadow. So, quick as a flash, I jumped off the lorry, 8×11."

$10 \times 8 = 80$

Inside the parcel was a note, a duster and some polish. The note read: "Dear Octavia, see what a mess your curiosity has got you into! I'm afraid only hard work can help you now. To get out of this box, you will have to polish the glass sides with the duster until they are so clean you can see the gold handle on the outside of the glass. When you see the handle, polish the floor just under that part of the glass, and you will discover a green button which opens the door. Good luck! W.W." Octavia had no idea who W.W. was. But suddenly she wished she had 11×8 legs. How many is that?

$8 \times 10 = 80$

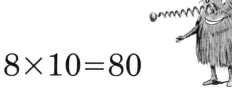

As Quentin's eyes grew used to the light, he saw rolling green fields stretching before him and tall towers in the distance. Dotted across the fields were strange animals with five horns – three on their heads and two on their bottoms. Quentin thought they looked very odd. In fact he was not sure which way round they were.

"Do you like our Booblegobs?" asked the Poggle.

"They're most unusual," said Quentin truthfully. "But what do you use them for?"

"They lay the grass, of course." Quentin gasped, but the Poggle only smiled. It pressed a button and a huge sail appeared above them and the wind carried them up into the air. All around, other Poggle trains were hurrying in different directions. The voice from the control panel said,

"Aboblegoodlegonk".

"Zeronk," answered the Poggle, and turned to Quentin. "We can land now." It turned a little handle and the sail came down. Gradually they floated to the ground. The glass dome slid open and the voice said,

"9×10 . . . you may leave the train now."

80

$9\times9=81$

By now Quentin felt he had heard rather a lot about Qat's lives, so he tried to change the subject.

"Ask me a question, Qat, and see if I can answer it."

"Certainly not," said Qat. "They say curiosity killed the cat, and I'm afraid I can't spare any more lives."

"Alright, I'll ask *you* one. What is a nought?"

"Why, a nought is nothing at all, you ninny," answered Qat scornfully.

"That means," Quentin went on, "that 10 is one-nothing, and 10×2 is 2 one-nothings and 10×9 is . . ."

$12 \times 7 = 84$

Stars flashed in front of Quentin's eyes, and he slid gently down the glass wall of the bubble. As he passed out, he caught a glimpse of Octavia the octopus floating by.

"I wish I knew more about that octopus," he thought.

He did find out more – on page 8.

$7 \times 12 = 84$

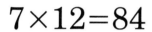

84 golden eagles flying across the sky like a swarm of giant locusts! Held in the claws of the leading eagle and waving down to him was his second son Shem.

"Shame on you, Shem," Noah shouted. "How could you do this to your old grey-haired father?" The eagle swooped right down until Shem's feet touched the ground and then let go of him very gently.

"Thanks, Goldie," he said to the eagle.

"Think nothing of it; you're as light as a feather," squawked the eagle, as he settled on the Ark.

"Hello Ham," Shem greeted his brother, "where's Japhet got to?" At that very moment they caught sight of 8×12 . . .

84

$11 \times 8 = 88$

Octavia grabbed the duster and started to clean one of the windows. Even though she had eight legs, it was only possible to clean one side at a time, because she only had one duster. How she wished she had a duster for each leg! She could hardly believe that she was wishing she could work harder.

She was just finishing the fifth glass wall, when suddenly she saw it: there it was, the gold handle! At once Octavia started polishing the floor. She felt so tired. Rub, rub, rub. All she wanted was 12 hours sleep for each of her eight legs. 12×8 . . . How many hours did she want?

$8 \times 11 = 88$

"I waited and waited by the side of the road. The sun was starting to set and I had to get back to you as quickly as possible. Luckily, another lorry came along just then, going in the direction of the beach. I managed to catch hold of the door and scramble into the cab. But the lorry was carrying a heavy load, and it slowed down as we reached a long, steep hill. Wasting no time, I jumped onto the speedometer and, in one bound, I turned 9 kilometres an hour into 9×11!"

10×9=90

"9 one-nothings, or should I say 90?" Qat was looking rather confused by this time. He decided to go on with his lives story.

"I'll tell you how I lost a life when I was quite a young kitten. I had terrible cat flu, so I was taken to the vet. She examined me carefully and then put a stethoscope to my chest.

'What is 11×9?' she asked kindly. The answer to that question is supposed to make rumbling noises in the chest so that the vet can tell what's wrong inside – but she didn't realize that I was too ill to do times tables. Do *you* know what 11×9 is?"

9×10=90

They had landed next to one of the towers.

"This is one of our living towers," the Poggle told Quentin as they passed several other Poggles coming and going. The inside of the tower was a great vaulted room with shiny walls the same colour as the Poggle's nose. Hundreds of brown furry armchairs were scattered around the room. Since the Poggles were also brown and furry, all you could see when a Poggle sat down were two large brown eyes.

"Come and look at this," said the Poggle pulling Quentin by the arm. On the wall was a large map with lots of flashing red lights all over it. "These are all the Poggles around the world having adventures in Poggle trains." Quentin was very impressed.

"Does this mean that none of them ever get lost?"

"That's right," answered the Poggle. "The round part at the end of our nose gives out a radio signal, so we are always in touch with Poggleland. Is it the same with your nose?"

"I'm afraid not," said Quentin, crinkling his nose and wishing it was a radio transmitter.

"Let's have something to eat," suggested the Poggle; leading him to a door marked 'Restaurant for Poggles and Friends Only. Say 10×10 to enter.'

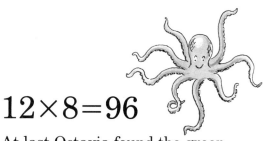

$12 \times 8 = 96$

At last Octavia found the green button. As she pressed it, the glass side slid open. She crawled out of the box, exhausted, and found her father and mother waiting for her.

"Well done, Octavia," cried her father. "That wasn't so bad was it?" Octavia promised herself that from now on she would try never to be lazy again. And her father decided to send the Wise Whale some of his seaweed sandwiches.

$8 \times 12 = 96$

96 snakes slithering towards them! Some headed straight for the gang-plank; others wound themselves round the ropes that secured the Ark and twisted themselves up like corkscrews. By now the Ark was getting crowded and the animals were beginning to squabble.

"There's not much room for more," observed Noah.

"I agree," replied Shem. "So where are we going to put that lot?" Noah turned to see 9×12 . . .

$11\times9=99$

"Ninety nine," answered Quentin brightly, but Qat had already begun to tell another story.

"I was once the head chef in a first class restaurant called The Cat's Whiskers," he boasted. "I was famous for miles around for some of my dishes. A particular favourite was a delicious fluffy pudding I made called mouse – or was it mousse? It's very simple to make. You take 12×9 mice . . ."

$9\times11=99$

99 kilometres an hour! Quentin was awestruck.

"That lorry had never moved so fast in its life. We shot back to the beach, and I rolled off onto the sand."

"But how did you get back to Quentin – oh dear, I mean to me?" asked Quentin.

"There was a big fat boy walking along carrying a surfboard, and I got a lift with the surfboard's shadow. You are rather long and thin, so I could hide behind it and not be seen. Off we went, looking like the answer to 10×11."

99

10×10=100

Inside the restaurant, the tables were shaped like bananas, and at each one sat two Poggles. Quentin and the Poggle found a table and the Poggle pressed a silver button. Part of the table slid away and a plate appeared with a card on it. It read: MENU

Speckled Eggs and Coconut Surprise

The Poggle pressed another silver button and two large speckled eggs appeared on the table before them. The Poggle leaned over politely,

"Would you care for a vegetarian egg?"

"How can you have vegetarian eggs?" asked the astonished Quentin.

"From the boolalong tree, of course." The Poggle pointed out of the window, and there in a field stood a magnificent, leafy tree. From its branches dangled clusters of the speckled eggs. Quentin cracked the shell of his egg and took a very small bite. It tasted just like chocolate mousse – it was fantastic! When they had finished, the coconut appeared. Eager to open it, Quentin turned it round and round, dropped it on the floor, and hit it with his spoon. The Poggle watched with amazement.

"I wonder if I can help," it said after some moments, taking the coconut from the struggling Quentin. "Try this. 11×10."

$12\times9=108$

"No, no!" cried Quentin. "I don't want to hear any more." He felt sure that Qat's pudding would not have agreed with him. "You've won the ninepins, Qat," he said quickly to change the subject, "but I challenge you to a return match when I come back from my holiday on page 10."

$9\times12=108$

108 lizards led by Japhet who looked particularly pleased with himself.

"Look how many lizards I've found," he gloated.

"I really don't see why you had to bring quite so many," his father replied irritably.

"Well, they've been in the world since the time of the dinosaurs and it didn't seem fair to miss them out. Then I got carried away."

"It will never float," said Noah. It was difficult to tell if he was crying because it was raining now and they were all rather wet.

"Oh, no," shouted Noah suddenly, "they can't all get in too!" But Japhet only smiled at 10×12 . . .

11×10=110

To Quentin's astonishment, the Poggle's nose twirled round and round like a drill and buried itself in the coconut. It emerged covered in white.

"Try some," the little creature smiled, offering Quentin the coconut, which now had a large hole in it. It was full of vanilla ice cream. Quentin could not remember when he'd last had such delicious food.

"If only mum made this at home," he thought. Suddenly he felt very homesick.

"Would you like to go now?" asked the Poggle with a knowing look.

"I think I would. I've been away quite a long time," Quentin admitted.

"Let's go then," said the Poggle kindly. "But first let me give you a present to remember Poggleland." It disappeared into a room marked 'Souvenir Shop' and came back with a long piece of shiny silk.

"What's it for?" asked Quentin.

"I don't really know," answered the Poggle. "But what I do know is that some children like to rub it gently against their faces at night. We call it a Schmeydrey."

"Thank you very much," said Quentin. They headed back to the Poggle train.

"12×10, enter," said the voice from the control panel.

10×11=110

"We reached the water's edge just as you were coming out. I was very pleased to see you because I was awfully hot and dusty after that trip. You, of course, took no notice. You started making sandcastles . . . Anyway, by then the light was fading and people began closing up their umbrellas. They stood stiffly in the sand, like a forest, while everyone packed their things. There must have been at least 11×11."

12 × 10 = 120

This time Quentin managed to strap himself in before they started. The concrete doors opened and the train moved forward. The doors closed behind them again and they were in darkness apart from the red glow of the control panel. Suddenly the green lights came on and the Poggle train shot off into the sea.

Quentin was very tired. He heard the Poggle counting backwards from ten, and his head fell gently onto the headrest. When he opened his eyes, he found himself back on his bed again. Dawn was breaking and the first rays of sunlight shone into his room. Quentin realized that it had all been a dream, but he couldn't help looking round for the Poggle's hole in the floor. There was no hole, only a book called 'Quentin's Mysterious Friend'. He opened it – and it started on page 11.

10 × 12 = 120

120 crocodiles heading towards them!

"No, I'm sorry," said Noah. "This is where I put my foot down." He stamped his foot and got completely covered in mud.

"But, Dad," wailed Japhet, "you told me to bring all the reptiles." Suddenly Noah's face lit up.

"I've got an idea," he shouted. "Quick, sons, go and get me as much rope as you can lay your hands on." Noah rushed into the Ark and grabbed a knife. Ham, Shem and Japhet each came back with 44 ropes and Noah cut each rope into three pieces. He found that 3×44 is the same as 11×12.

120

$11\times11=121$

"At last it was time to go home. I had grown rather long by then and was extremely tired, so I hid in the shadow of the umbrella your dad was carrying which saved me walking all the way back."

"Lucky you," said Quentin, thinking that he too must have been very tired that evening.

"Oh, I can usually find somewhere to hide," the shadow boasted. "For instance, a long number is always a useful place."

"I know, I know," Quentin smiled, "something like 12×11."

12×11=132

"Exactly. Nobody would ever think of looking for me at 132. In fact, most people forget that 132 is the end of the 11 times table. Anyway, next time you are enjoying yourself, please remember me."

"I promise," said Quentin solemnly. At that moment, the sitting room door opened and the light from the hall flooded the room. Quentin looked round, but the shadow had vanished. All that was left was a voice repeating faintly, "Remember me . . . remember me!" Quentin picked up a book, and opened it at page 12.

11×12=132

Noah had 132 pieces of rope. Before his sons could stop him, he rushed up to the first crocodile and bent over it. The crocodile leapt up at him with its jaws wide open and tried to bite him. Noah quickly lashed a rope round its mouth and tied a knot over the snout. He fastened the end of the rope securely to the side of the Ark. Then he grabbed another rope and did the same thing to another crocodile.

"What are you doing, Dad?" asked Ham, who thought his father must be going mad.

"If we tie all the crocodiles to the Ark, they can keep us afloat and pull us along when the water is deep enough," he explained. "Quick, come and help me before it's too late." The four of them grabbed ropes and managed to tie all the crocodiles to the Ark. But only just in time. By now they really needed their boots – the water was deeper and the crocodiles were starting swimming practice.

"Into the Ark," shouted Noah. "The end is coming!" And so it was, because 12×12 is . . .

$12 \times 12 = 144$

. . . which, as you know, is the last of the times tables.

Noah and his sons managed to get into the Ark in time. The crocodiles did a great job. They were helped by the elephants who stuck their trunks out of the windows and blew into the water. It was the first jet-propelled boat in history. Finally they landed on a mountain. After how many days?

Was it 144? I don't think so really, do you?